EYE ON THE SKY

WHEN LIGHTNING STRIKES

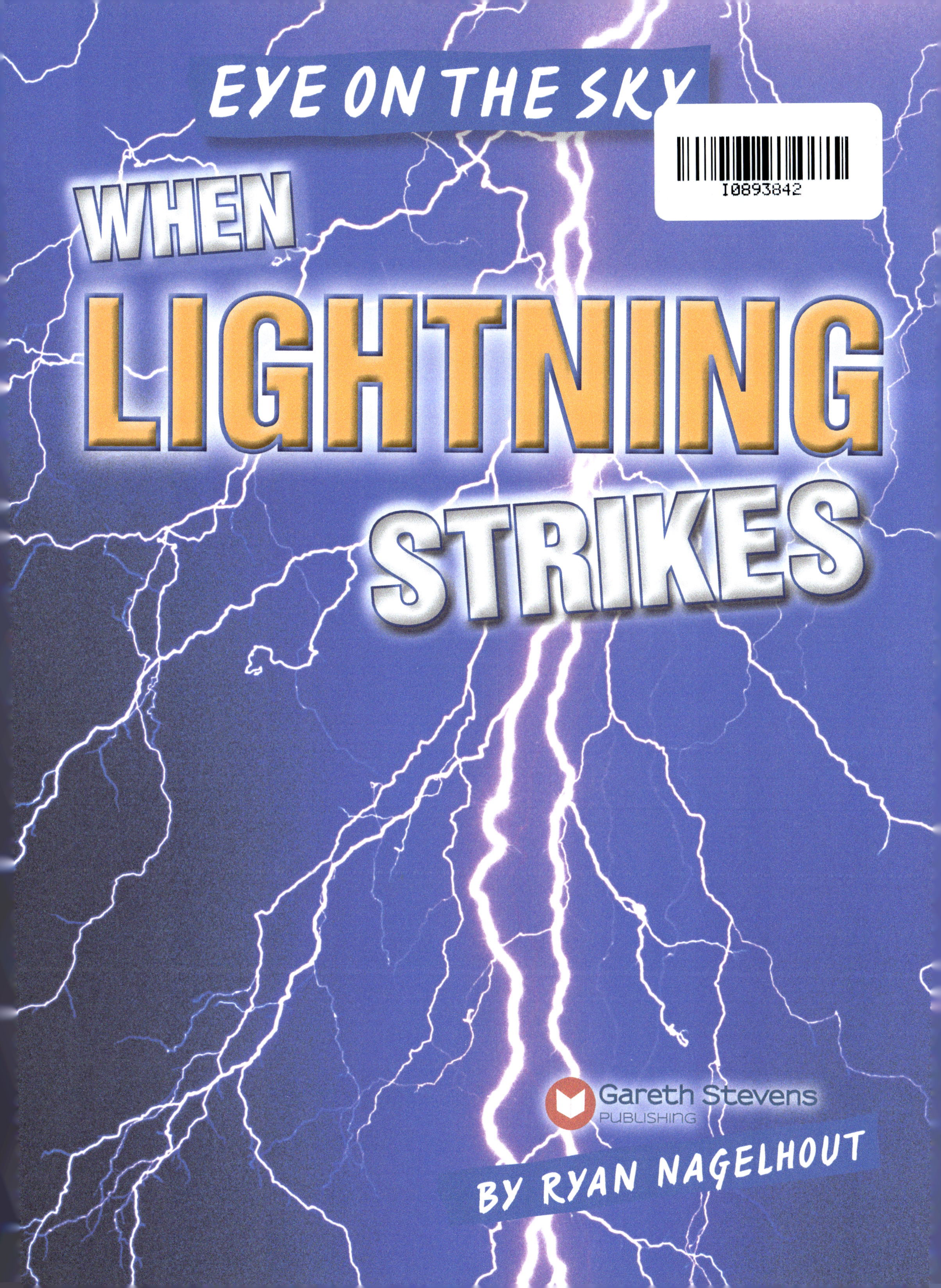

Gareth Stevens PUBLISHING

BY RYAN NAGELHOUT

Please visit our website, www.garethstevens.com. For a free color catalog of all our high-quality books, call toll free 1-800-542-2595 or fax 1-877-542-2596.

Cataloging-in-Publication Data

Nagelhout, Ryan.
When lightning strikes / by Ryan Nagelhout.
p. cm. — (Eye on the sky)
Includes index.
ISBN 978-1-4824-2892-6 (pbk.)
ISBN 978-1-4824-2893-3 (6 pack)
ISBN 978-1-4824-2894-0 (library binding)
1. Lightning — Juvenile literature. 2. Thunderstorms — Juvenile literature. I. Nagelhout, Ryan. II. Title.
QC966.5 N34 2016
551.56'32—d23

Published in 2016 by
Gareth Stevens Publishing
111 East 14th Street, Suite 349
New York, NY 10003

Designer: Laura Bowen
Editor: Kristen Rajczak

Photo credits: Cover, p. 1 Ralph Wetmore/Stone/Getty Images; cover, pp. 1–32 (series art) Nik Merkulov/Shutterstock.com; p. 5 Cultura Science/Jason Persoff Stormdoctor/Stone/Getty Images; p. 7 kazoka/Shutterstock.com; p. 8 S-F/Shutterstock.com; p. 10 Scott Olson/Getty Images News/Getty Images; p. 11 Richard A. Brooks/AFP/Getty Images; p. 13 miamia/Shutterstock.com; p. 15 brimkelly/Shutterstock.com; p. 17 Education Images/Universal Images Group/Getty Images; p. 18 Joe Thomissen/Wikimedia Commons, p. 19 Wild Horizon/Universal Images Group/Getty Images; p. 21 Mike Lyvers/Moment/Getty Images; p. 23 (forked) Piotr Krzeslak/Shutterstock.com; p. 23 (intercloud) aco/Shutterstock.com; p. 23 (sheet) Sahachat Saneha/Shutterstock.com; p. 25 Justin Sullivan/Getty Images News/Getty Images; p. 27 Miroslav Fechtner/Shutterstock.com; p. 29 Boston Globe/Getty Images.

Printed in the United States of America

CPSIA compliance information: Batch #CS15GS: For further information contact Gareth Stevens, New York, New York at 1-800-542-2595.

CONTENTS

Words in the glossary appear in **bold** type the first time they are used in the text.

THE GATHERING STORM

Nine-year-old Alexander Hermann was getting ready for his first day of soccer practice in Bee Cave, Texas, when **disaster** struck. Just before practice started, a huge boom shook the soccer field. Then there was the sound of people calling for help.

Alexander fell to the ground and wasn't breathing. Was he struck by lightning? The sky was a mix of sun and clouds. How could lightning strike in those conditions? Carson Monks, a 19-year-old soccer coach, saved Alexander's life by performing **CPR** until he started breathing again. But could they have known a strike was coming? And what exactly is lightning, anyway?

EVERY SECOND COUNTS

There are about 2,000 thunderstorms going on all around the world right now. During those thunderstorms, there are about 100 lightning strikes every second. That may sound scary, but understanding what lightning is and why it happens will prepare you for the next time a storm comes through your neighborhood.

A storm was still miles away in 2014 when Alexander was struck. So how was he hit? Read on to find out!

THE BRIGHT LIGHT

Lightning is a giant **discharge** of electricity. It creates a bright flash of light and heat along with a large noise called thunder. It's a natural event that happens when the attraction, or pull, of opposite electrical charges is strong enough to overcome the **resistance** created by air.

Storms with clouds that create lightning are called thunderstorms. Clouds form when water vapor condenses high above Earth. The towering clouds of a thunderstorm, called cumulonimbus clouds, can grow up to 39,000 feet (12,000 m) above Earth. Water vapor inside these clouds often **condenses** and freezes. Bits of ice and water in the clouds bump into each other and become electrically charged.

NATURE'S FURY

Lightning is the leading cause of weather-related death and injury in the United States. Almost every kind of natural disaster—hurricanes, tornadoes, and bad thunderstorms—creates lightning of some kind. There's about a 1 in 3,000 chance you'll be struck by lightning in your lifetime! At least 26 people in the United States died after being struck by lightning in 2014.

Lightning usually looks white or yellow, but its color depends on the colors in the sky when it strikes.

TOP TO BOTTOM

As electrical charges are created, they arrange themselves in the cloud by type. Positive charges, or protons, gather at the top of the cumulonimbus cloud. Negative charges, or electrons, gather in the center of the cumulonimbus cloud. A small number of protons also group together at the very bottom of the cloud.

TWICE, THRICE, AND MORE

Don't believe the myth that lightning never strikes the same place twice. It can, and will, strike places more than once, especially tall buildings and large trees. The Burj Khalifa in Dubai, United Arab Emirates, is the tallest building in the world. It can be struck dozens of times during a single storm!

Opposite electrical charges attract one another. Cloud-to-ground lightning starts in thunderclouds as the negative charges in the middle are drawn to the lower part of the cloud. This movement of charges creates a channel of ionized air—air made of **neutral** atoms that take on an electrical charge.

About one-third of lightning is between a cloud and the ground, starting in the negatively charged part of the cloud.

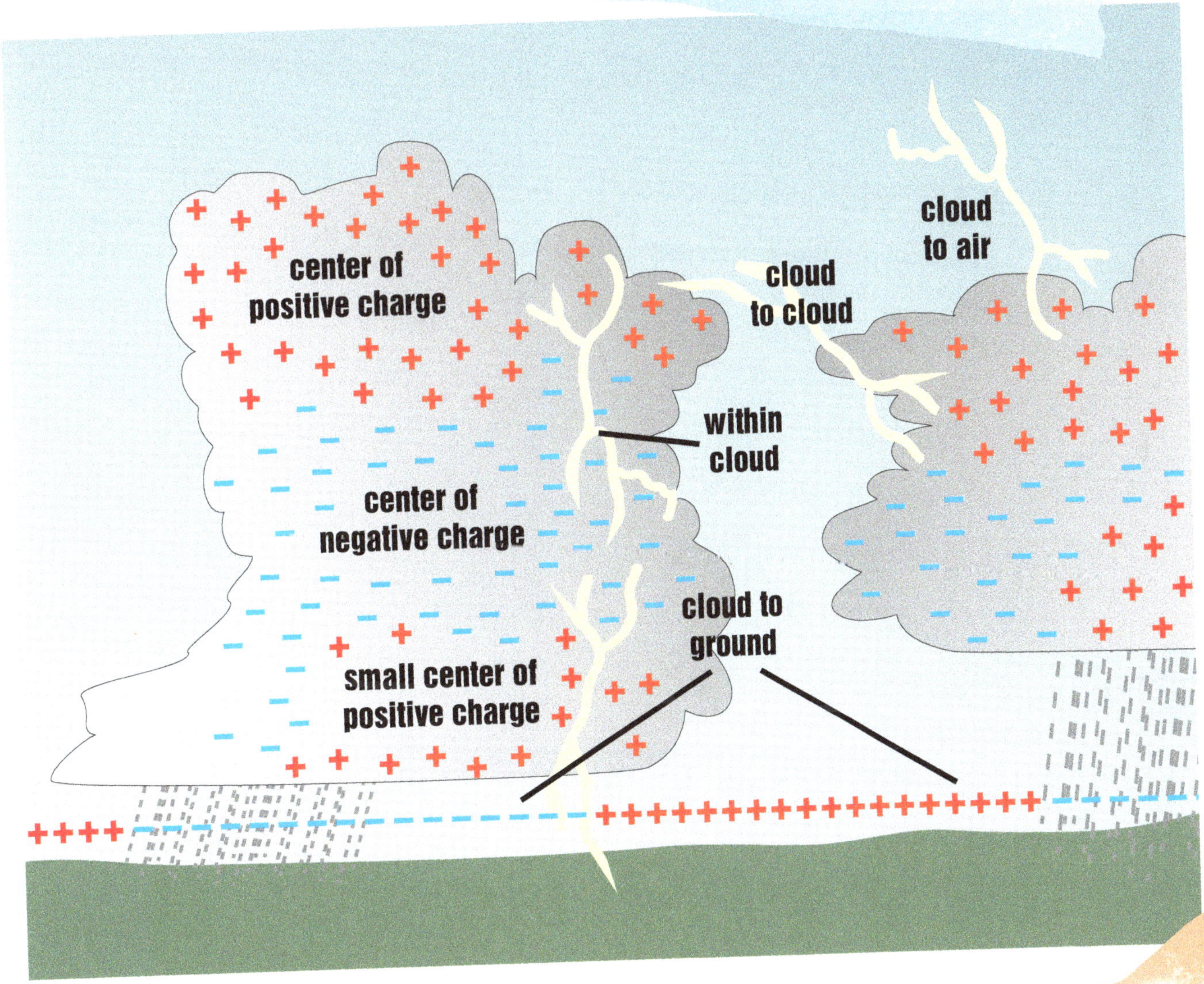

Ionized air creates the basic path a cloud-to-ground lightning strike follows. A first lightning stroke, called a leader, moves down toward the ground. Leaders are usually negatively charged. When the leader reaches about 100 feet (30 m) above the ground, a discharge of the opposite charge reaches up from the ground to meet it. The cloud is now connected to the ground, and a bright return stroke shoots back up to the cloud.

This back and forth happens extremely quickly: the leader stroke reaches the ground in just milliseconds (one thousandths of a second), and the return stroke hits the cloud in about 100 microseconds (one millionths of a second)!

JUST HOW HOT?

A bolt of lightning is no more than an inch (2.5 cm) wide. Lightning strikes are extremely hot, even hotter than the surface of the sun! Return strokes can reach temperatures of 50,000°F (28,000°C). These extremely hot bolts can turn sand to glass and even affect the gases in air.

A typical lightning strike will have three or four return strokes in it.

THUNDER WORKS

Thunder is caused by lightning strikes. When lightning moves from a cloud to the ground, the bolt makes a channel in the air that's heated to a high temperature so quickly that pressure builds up and compresses the air. When the light and energy are gone, the air contracts. This rapid change in air pressure creates the sound we call thunder!

Lightning travels at about one-third the speed of light. Sound travels much slower, and its speed is affected by the height above sea level. So although thunder and lightning happen at nearly the same time, we don't hear thunder until after a lightning strike.

WHAT TOOK YOU SO LONG?

You can actually use thunder to measure how far away from you lightning struck! Count the number of seconds between when you see lightning and hear the thunder. Then divide by five. The number you have left is how many miles away the bolt struck. You can multiply that number by 1.6 to find the distance in kilometers.

Often you can see lightning and not hear thunder because it's too far away. This is sometimes called heat lighting because it often appears on hot days with few clouds in the sky.

HAIR-RAISING STORIES

On August 20, 1975, Sean McQuilken and his family hiked to the top of Moro Rock in Sequoia National Park in California. As they reached the top, they noticed dark clouds overhead and light rain starting to fall.

His sister, Mary, took a funny photo of Sean and their brother Michael with their hair standing on end. Minutes later, the temperature dropped, and it started to hail. On the way down the mountain, Sean and another hiker were struck by lightning! The other hiker was killed, while Sean and his clothes were badly burned.

CHARGES IN THE AIR

The McQuilkens' hair standing on end was a sign that lightning would soon strike. Hair stands on end near thunderstorms when positive charges are rising through a person and toward a negatively charged thundercloud. If you ever feel your hair stand on end before or during a storm, get inside! Lightning could strike soon.

Moro Rock rises 6,725 feet (2,050 m) above sea level. Hikers and climbers should be careful at the top of such a landform if a storm is coming.

OUT OF THE BLUE

Gretel Ehrlich was walking a mile (1.6 km) away from black storm clouds when thunder scared her two dogs. The next thing she knew, Ehrlich was on the ground bleeding, unable to swallow, talk, or move her legs. Much like Alexander Hermann's brush with lightning, Ehrlich said she didn't think lightning would strike from so far away. So what happened?

These two strikes could have been something called positive, or anvil, lightning. This is lightning that comes from the top of a thundercloud. It carries a positive charge and can reach as far as 10 miles (16 km) away from the cloud.

QUICK BOLTS

There are many stories about lightning strikes happening far from the rain and winds of a big thunderstorm. Lightning can strike in places where skies are clear. The bolts come from clouds that look very far off in the distance. It's important to remember that a "bolt from the blue" is possible if clouds are within 5 to 10 miles (8 to 16 km).

Ehrlich's two dogs were right to be spooked by that thunder. A bolt of lightning came rushing out of a cloud to meet them from far away!

GREAT BALLS OF... LIGHTNING?

One of the freakiest types of lightning is called ball lightning. Ball lightning is so rare many scientists didn't believe it was possible until they saw it for themselves. A group of scientists saw ball lightning move through their airplane once! Another scientist saw a glowing, tennis ball-sized mass of energy floating near him when he was 16.

Ball lightning is said to make a hissing noise and often makes a loud crackle when it explodes! Ball lightning can get as big as a beach ball. It only lasts a few seconds, but touching it can be deadly!

KILLED BY A BALL

At least one scientist is thought to have been killed by ball lightning. Georg Richmann was **electrocuted** by ball lightning in 1753 in St. Petersburg, Russia. Richmann was working on an experiment involving a lightning rod, which is a large metal pole used to attract lightning to a particular place.

The most common kind of lightning happens inside a cloud between the positive and negative charges.

VOLCANO LIGHTNING?

Volcanic eruptions are dangerous natural events that can cause massive **damage** to nature and people living nearby. But did you know they can also cause lightning strikes? Scientists studying Redoubt, an active volcano in Alaska, discovered that a large volcanic **plume** can spark thousands of lighting bolts in storms that last more than an hour. These bolts even struck more than 93 miles (150 km) **downwind** from the eruption!

Scientists say matter coming out of a volcano has a positive charge, which attracts negatively charged matter in clouds and makes lightning more likely.

JOHNSTOWN FLOOD

Scientists think volcanoes can create different kinds of lightning. More **intense** bolts are formed near the eruption itself by positively charged liquid rock and other matter escaping Earth. However, scientists also think **particles** in the plumes being carried by wind bounce off one another and create charges that spark lightning just like in clouds!

More lightning can be seen at the beginning of eruptions, so it's hard to photograph it while staying safe!

THUNDERSNOW AND MORE

Cloud-to-ground lightning is the most dangerous kind of lightning to people, but there are many different kinds of lightning strikes. Some lightning moves from one cloud to another, which doesn't affect people below at all!

One particularly crazy kind of storm drops snow in addition to creating lightning and thunder. These storms are often called thundersnow. Long, flat snow clouds have bulges that rise quickly and make the air in the cloud unstable. The snowflakes and tiny balls of snow called graupel in these spots create electrical charges that result in lightning strikes!

ST. ELMO'S FIRE

For centuries, sailors have told of a blue and green glow on the front of their ships during or after a bad thunderstorm. Called St. Elmo's Fire, it occurs when tiny positively charged sparks respond to negative charges in the air or clouds. Sailors thought it was a sign of good luck, meaning they survived a bad storm without losing the ship.

Here are a few different types of lightning scientists have studied.

ANVIL LIGHTNING—lightning from the top of a thundercloud that strikes an area with clear skies

BALL LIGHTNING—very rare globes of lightning that float, hiss, and explode

CHAIN LIGHTNING—broken lightning bolts that fade into dotted lines

CLOUD-TO-GROUND LIGHTNING—bolts that move from a cloud overhead to Earth

FORKED LIGHTNING—lightning bolts that split into a number of branches

INTERCLOUD LIGHTNING—lightning strikes traveling between clouds

INTRACLOUD LIGHTNING—flashes within a cloud that has both positive and negative particles

RIBBON LIGHTNING—lightning separated by wind that streaks the sky

SHEET LIGHTNING—flashes of light that illuminate entire clouds

THUNDERSNOW—lightning and thunder created in low-lying winter snow clouds

forked lightning

intercloud lightning

sheet lightning

MORE STRIKES COMING?

Researchers think the United States will see about a 50 percent rise in lightning strikes over the next century. This is because of global climate change. Scientists think we will see more lightning because a warmer atmosphere can hold more moisture, which helps create lightning strikes.

This is dangerous because while lightning can hurt humans, it also causes wildfires when lightning strikes dry brush or trees in a forest, setting them on fire. Wildfires often happen in dry seasons in states such as California and can destroy many homes and animal habitats.

GREENHOUSE GASES

More lightning strikes would further impact the gases in our atmosphere. This would be good and bad for our climate. Greenhouse gases in Earth's atmosphere trap heat, a major part of climate change. More lightning means more of a greenhouse gas called ozone. However, lightning also creates nitrogen oxide, which helps reduce levels of the greenhouse gas methane.

Scientists think intense forest fires can actually cause lightning strikes!

STAYING SAFE

If you see lightning or tall thunderclouds in the distance, the best thing you can do to stay safe is get inside. Keep away from and close all doors and windows. Getting inside a house or a car is always the best option.

If you're outdoors, go to a building or a car. Don't stand under a tree, baseball dugouts, or bleachers. These are places that may attract lightning strikes. Don't go swimming during a lightning storm. Water is a good conductor of electricity, and you may be the highest point lightning can use to meet the ground.

WHEN LIGHTNING STRIKES

If you're inside:

- avoid doors and windows.
- avoid metal or water.
- stay off the phone.
- unplug computers and TVs.

If you're outside:

- go inside, find other shelter, or crouch down with feet together and hands over ears.
- don't stand in puddles.
- don't swim.
- stay away from groups of people.
- avoid trees and tall, metal objects.

FEELING A SURGE

Some people use a strip of power plugs called a surge protector for their electronic devices. However, surge protectors don't protect electronic things from direct lightning strikes. Be sure to unplug any valuable electronics, such as computers or TVs, before lightning strikes. Lightning can do lots of electrical damage to homes and businesses with a direct hit.

Most people hurt by lightning when inside their homes are talking on their telephone! Stay away from anything that conducts electricity during a storm.

AFTER THE STORM

Cleaning up after an intense thunderstorm can take a long time. Lightning storms bring heavy rain and hail and can create quite a mess, including fallen trees, branches, and downed power lines. Lightning strikes can cause electrical damage to homes and businesses and even start fires.

However, the most important thing is making sure you're safe. If you or a friend is struck by lightning, call for help immediately. The best way to prevent lightning injuries is to watch the sky for trouble. If you see lightning, get inside and get ready for a storm. If you can hear thunder, lightning can strike nearby!

HOW DO YOU SURVIVE?

How do so many people survive lightning strikes? Well, lightning isn't interested in staying in someone's body long enough to kill them. The strike is only meant to balance electrical charges on Earth. Lightning is just the quickest, scariest way nature has to balance things out, and sometimes people get in the way!

People struck by lightning can have heart attacks, suffer burns, and often have nerve damage.

GLOSSARY

condense: to lose heat and change from a gas into a liquid

CPR: also called cardiopulmonary resuscitation, a method of restarting a person's heartbeat and breathing

damage: harm, or to cause harm

disaster: an event that causes much suffering or loss

discharge: to set free or release

downwind: in the direction the wind is blowing

electrocute: to kill by electric shock

intense: existing in an extreme degree

neutral: having no charge

particle: a very small piece of something

plume: something such as smoke, steam, or water that rises into the air in a tall, thin shape

resistance: the opposition or prevention of something

volcanic eruption: the bursting forth of hot, liquid rock from within Earth

FOR MORE INFORMATION

BOOKS

Edison, Erin. *Lightning.* Mankato, MN: Capstone Press, 2012.

Herriges, Ann. *Lightning.* Minneapolis, MN: Bellwether Media, 2007.

Owings, Lisa. *What Protects Us During Natural Disasters?* Minneapolis, MN: Lerner Publications, 2016.

WEBSITES

Flash Facts About Lightning
news.nationalgeographic.com/news/2004/06/0623_040623_lightningfacts.html
Learn more facts about lightning strikes on this National Geographic website.

Lightning Map
lightningmaps.org/realtime
Watch lightning strike all around the world in real time on this map.

Lightning Safety
www.lightningsafety.noaa.gov/
Find out more information about staying safe during lightning storms on the official site of the National Weather Service.

Publisher's note to educators and parents: Our editors have carefully reviewed these websites to ensure that they are suitable for students. Many websites change frequently, however, and we cannot guarantee that a site's future contents will continue to meet our high standards of quality and educational value. Be advised that students should be closely supervised whenever they access the Internet.

INDEX